On Target English

Sentence and Word Skills

Year 3

Hilary Frost
Sarah Lindsay
Heather Painter

SOUTH VIEW
COMMUNITY
PRIMARY SCHOOL

Longman

Edinburgh Gate
Harlow, Essex

Contents

	Sentence	Word	Handwriting
Unit 11 page 34 Firefighters to the Rescue	comparing adjectives capital letters in titles	*ph* words suffixes *ful, less*	horizontal joins to letters without ascenders – *ou, ow*
Unit 12 page 37 Saint George and the Dragon	collective nouns capital letters for proper nouns	*are, ere* words contractions	horizontal joins to letters without ascenders – *wa*
Unit 13 page 40 The Good Friend	singular and plural sentences using *am, are, is*	silent letters antonyms	horizontal joins to letters without ascenders – *wr*
Unit 14 page 43 Making a Musical Instrument	overworked words editing	*er, ir, ur* words dictionary work	diagonal joins to letters with ascenders – *al, ul*
Unit 15 page 46 Gulliver's Travels	using *did, done* writing letters	*str* words adding *y*	diagonal joins to letters with ascenders – *ch*
Unit 16 page 49 The Tale of Thomas Mead	pronouns speech marks	*ea* words dialogue words	diagonal joins to letters with ascenders – *et, it*
Unit 17 page 52 Children in Roman Times	possessive pronouns conjunctions *but, and*	*ch* words dictionary work	horizontal joins to letters with ascenders – *old*
Unit 18 page 55 Superpooch	gender words speech marks and commas	*ear, ead* words homonyms	horizontal joins to letters with ascenders – *wh*
Unit 19 page 58 Fun Poems	personal pronouns capital letters in poetry	double letters adding *er* to root words	horizontal joins to letters with ascenders – *oth*
Unit 20 page 61 Road Accident	pronouns and contractions using conjunctions	*igh* words expressions	horizontal joins to letters with ascenders – *ol*

3

The Tale of Brave Augustus

Sentence work

- To understand and use verbs

Remember

Verbs are sometimes called **doing** words.

Helpful words

swims on the pond
eats the weeds
flaps his wings
cleans his feathers

Verbs

Augustus <u>swims</u> on the pond.
Words, like **swims**, that tell us about actions, are called **verbs**.

1 What is Augustus doing? Write a sentence for each picture.
Underline the verb in each one.

a Augustus <u>swims</u> on the pond.

b

c

d

2 Write one sentence about what Mrs Popple is doing. Underline the action verb.

Capital letters and full stops

 Sentence work

● To practise using capital letters and full stops

1 Copy these sentences about Mrs Popple. Put in the capital letters and full stops.

mrs popple lived in a little white cottage

in the garden mrs popple grew potatoes onions cabbages and carrots

there were flowers each side of the path

on the pond lived augustus, mrs popple's large white gander

 Remember

Every sentence must start with a **capital letter** and end with a **full stop**.
Proper nouns start with capital letters, too.

2 Write your own sentence about Augustus.

old words

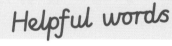 **Word work**

● To learn to spell words with *old*

old Mrs Popple

1 Write an *old* word to match each picture:

Helpful words

sold gold fold
cold hold bold

a

b

c

d

e

f

2 Add *ing* to one of the words you have written in question 1. Put the word in a sentence.

Word work

- To learn to spell words with *le*

Words ending in *le*

Mrs Popple lived in a little white cottage.

1 Look carefully at the puzzle box.
List all the words ending in *le*.

 Tip

In the puzzle box, some words go across and some go down.

a	f	t	h	i	s	t	l	e
h	b	o	v	r	h	k	a	n
g	r	r	j	g	s	t	d	c
c	a	n	d	l	e	j	b	h
p	m	k	l	t	s	o	a	k
g	b	u	h	s	n	t	n	k
y	l	e	f	n	y	v	g	f
r	e	c	t	a	n	g	l	e
d	o	k	n	u	e	s	e	d

2 Write three words with *le* endings that are not in the puzzle box.

 Handwriting

Letter patterns

ol ol ol ol ol ol ol ol ol ol ol ol ol ol ol

Old Mrs Popple is cold

1 Copy the *ol* letter pattern.

2 Copy this neatly:

Mrs Popple sold her old, cold cottage.

6

A Snowy Morning

Choosing verbs

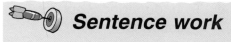

- To use action verbs

We use **different verbs** for **different sorts of actions**.

tiptoed downstairs

walked downstairs

ran downstairs

1 Write a *moving about* verb to match each picture:

hop

a

b

c

d

e

Remember

Verbs are **action** or **doing** words.

Helpful words

Some *moving about* verbs:
hop run skip walk chase rush sprint creep crawl

2 Look at one or two pages in your reading book. Copy all the *action* verbs that you can find.

Sentence work

- To understand what a question is

Tip

?
■

Can you see the **full stop** at the bottom of the **question mark**?

Asking questions

Has icy cold air ever brought tears to your eyes?

This sentence asks a **question**.
Questions end with a **?**

1 Copy only the question sentences.
Add the missing capital letters and question marks.

was jenny awake when the sun rose
what did she see through her window
pumpkins grew in the field
why did jenny tiptoe about

2 Write a question for your friend to answer.

Word work

- To learn to spell words with *air* and *ear*

Tip

Say the words. Listen to the sound the letters *air* and *ear* make.

Helpful words

bear hear hair
wear pear near
pair chair fear

air and *ear* words

air and *ear* sometimes sound the same:	Sometimes they make a different sound:
h**air** w**ear**	**air** t**ear**s

The icy air brought tears to her eyes...

1 Write a word for each gap:

Our baby pulled my _____ as I sat on the _____ to pull on my boots.
She ran off with my _____ of slippers with the teddy _____ on.
Mum said I should _____ the red _____ of boots to school in the thick snow.

2 Write three columns of words:

air words	ear (wear) words	ear (fear) words
chair	pear	clear

Prefixes

A **prefix** is added to the beginning of a word.
Adding the prefixes **un** and **dis** can change words to their opposite meaning.

Jess was <u>happy</u> when her class was allowed to play in the snow.

Sam was <u>unhappy</u> when his class was not!

1 Add *un* or *dis* to each of these words:

__happy   __appear

__tie   __like

__even   __obey

2 Write a sentence with an **un** word, and another with a **dis** word.

Letter patterns

Our baby can crawl

1 Copy the **wl** letter pattern.

2 Add *awl* to these letters to make some words:

crawl   br____   sh____   b____

Word work

- To learn the prefixes *un* and *dis*

Remember

Words that have **opposite** meanings are called **antonyms**.

Helpful words

unhappy   untie
uneven   disobey
dislike   disappear

Handwriting

Unusual Poems

 Remember

Verbs are sometimes called **doing** or **action** words.

Choosing verbs

They'll just bring in a lawn mower and <u>cut</u> you down short.

Instead of **cut** we could write:

slice   chop   hack   mow

Thinking carefully about the **verbs** can make our writing more interesting.

1 Sort the verbs in the box into the correct columns.

chewed   bit   walked   dawdled   munched
replied   shouted   called   gobbled   ran
whispered   chased   asked   sprinted   ate

Moving about verbs	Speaking verbs	Eating verbs

2 Copy each sentence and change the underlined verb for one that is more interesting:

"Whoever made the pillowcases pink?" <u>said</u> Mum.

I <u>ate</u> my food and went out before the others came home.

I <u>went</u> round to Gran's house as quickly as I could.

Full stops and question marks

1 In this poem about a launderette, the poet has left out the full stops and question marks.

Copy the poem, putting in the missing punctuation marks to show that you know where the sentences end.

> My washing's going round and round I left that red sock in It's dyeing Matthew's shirt and Ian's football kit He'll kill me What will Mum say about the pink pillowcases I'll say the lady put them in for me Yes that's what I'll say

2 Write a sentence that needs a question mark.

oo and *u* words

Ian's football kit was put in the full washing machine.

Sometimes the letters **oo** and **u** make the same sounds.

1 Add the rhyming word:

soot rhymes with _foot_

pull rhymes with _____

cook rhymes with _____

hood rhymes with _____

fully rhymes with _____

rook rhymes with _____

2 Write as many words as you can that rhyme with **cook**.

 Sentence work

● To practise using full stops and question marks

 Tip

The capital letters have been put in to help you.

 Word work

● To learn to spell words with *oo* and *u*

Tip

Say the words. Listen to the sound the letters **oo** and **u** make.

Helpful words

wood hook
bully foot
bull book

11

Word work

- To understand synonyms

Helpful words

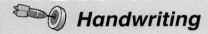

*stiff jolly express
huge quick glad
speedy cross large
tell mad firm*

Synonyms

Words like this with similar meanings are called **synonyms**.
When we write poems we often need to find a different word with a similar meaning.

1 Write two synonyms for:

happy   hard   say

big   angry   fast

2 Make a list of as many synonyms as you can for:

good   nice

Handwriting

Letter patterns

ot ot ot ot ot ot ot ot ot ot ot ot ot ot ot

Shot!

1 Copy the **ot** letter pattern.

2 a Add *oot* to these letters to make words:

f__oot__ball   *h_____*   *sh_____*

     b_____   *r_____*

b Copy this neatly:

Shoot it, don't just boot it!

12

Little Red Riding Hood Goes to Town

Past tense

 Sentence work

- To understand and use verbs in the past tense

> If a verb ends with **ed**, it has happened in the **past**:
>
> happen happen**ed**   move mov**ed**
>
> *What happen<u>ed</u> when Little Red Riding Hood moved to the town?*

1 Write these verbs in the past tense.
The first is done to help you.

play   live   walk   love   look

played

Tip

If a verb ends with **e**, just add **d** to make the past tense.

2 Write these sentences in the past tense.
Fill each gap by choosing a verb from
the box, and adding **d** or **ed** to it.

> want   agree   visit   live   like

Little Red Riding Hood _____ in the forest.

She _____ living in the forest.

Her mother _____ to move to the town.

Little Red Riding Hood _____ it would be sensible.

She _____ her new flat.

Sentence work

● To use commas in a list

Writing lists

We use commas between each item in a list, but we use **and** between the last two.

From her bedroom Little Red Riding Hood could see the roofs of houses, flats, offices, many big factories, the hospital, a multiplex cinema, a shopping centre, three churches <u>and</u> a mosque.

1 Copy these sentences.
Put in the missing commas and full stops.

Little Red Riding Hood knew she would miss the trees wild flowers animals fresh air and the wide open spaces

Living in a town meant she could go shopping go to the swimming pool visit the cinema and meet lots of new friends

2 Write a sentence, naming some things you might find in Little Red Riding Hood's bedroom.

Word work

● To learn to spell words with *ow* and *ou*

Helpful words

shouting scout houses
clouds mouse cow
town crowd
clown growling

ow and *ou* words

1 Look at the picture.
List all the **ow** and **ou** words you can see.

2 Copy the table. Put the words you have found in it.

Words with <u>ow</u>	Words with <u>ou</u>

What does it mean?

When we are reading, we don't always understand what a word means.
Pictures can give a clue, and so can the rest of the sentence.

Red Riding Hood was dismayed and sorry that her balcony was quite so far above the ground.

Word work

● To look for clues to help understand words

Tip

Dismayed means unhappy.

A **balcony** is a platform high above the ground.

1 Write what you think each **bold** word means. Look for clues.

Little Red Riding Hood could see the new bridge being built **beyond** the town centre.

She watched the **construction** workers.

One man was **descending** a tall ladder.

2 Use the word *disappointed* in a sentence about Little Red Riding Hood.

Letter patterns

owl owl owl owl owl owl owl

Howl! Howl!

1 Copy the *owl* letter pattern.

2 **a** Add *owl* to these letters to make some words:

fowl   h_____   gr_____

     pr_____   sc_____

b Copy this neatly:

The owl saw the big, bad wolf howl and growl and then prowl up and down.

Handwriting

The Olympics

Sentence work

- To understand and use verbs in the present and past tense

Tip

When we talk about verbs, another word for *time* is **tense**.

Verbs – present and past

If something is *happening now*, it is happening at the **present** time:

*The swimmers are trai**ning** for the Olympics.*

If something has *already happened*, it happened in the **past**:

*The first Olympic Games happen**ed** 3000 years ago.*

1 Copy the two lists.
Draw a line to join the matching **present** tense and **past** tense verbs.

present	past
jumping	asked
training	happened
happening	shouted
asking	trained
shouting	jumped

2 Write these sentences, as if they had happened in the **past**, using a verb ending in *ed*:

Tom is jumping well.

The weight-lifter is lifting more than his own weight.

Our oarsmen are rowing in the final.

The crowd are shouting loudly.

Helpful words

shouted   rowed
jumped   lifted

16

Speech bubbles

On your marks.

Wait! I'm not ready.

Come on Nilesh, come on son!

The words in the **speech bubbles** were spoken.

1 What did each of these people say:
- the starter?
- the swimmer?
- Nilesh's father?

2 What do you think the starter said next?

ar words

start

mark

arm

1 Find four words for each rhyming set:
- **art** words *start*
- **ark** words *mark*
- **arm** words *arm*

2 Choose a word from each rhyming set and use it in a sentence.

 **Sentence work**

- To pick out words spoken

 Word work

- To learn to spell words with *ar*

Helpful words

dart park farm
arm mark start
dark cart harm
part bark alarm

17

Word work

- To understand how words change when *ing* is added

Remember

The **vowel letters** are
a e i o u.

Handwriting

Adding *ing*

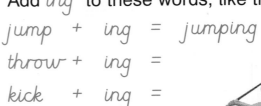 

1 Add *ing* to these words, like this:

jump + ing = jumping
throw + ing =
kick + ing =
sprint + ing =
pull + ing =

If there is a vowel letter *before* the last letter, the last letter is sometimes *doubled* before adding *ing*:

swim   swimming
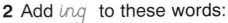

2 Add *ing* to these words:

hit + ing = hitting
hop + ing =
win + ing =
bat + ing =
slip + ing =

Letter patterns

rt rt rt rt rt rt rt rt rt rt rt rt rt rt rt rt

A smart cart

1 Copy the **rt** letter pattern.

2 a Add *art* to these letters to make some words:

cart   sm_____   d_____   st_____   p_____

b Copy this neatly:

It was nearly dark in the park before they could start.

18

Time to Get Up!

Verbs – present and past

Remember, we often add **ed** to a verb to tell our reader if something happened in the **past**:

shout   shout<u>ed</u>

Some verbs have to be changed into a new word:

go   <u>went</u>

make   <u>made</u>

say   <u>said</u>

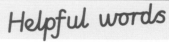 ***Sentence work***

● To practise using verbs in the past tense

1 Write a matching past tense verb for each of these:

find <u>found</u>   hold   drink   eat

make   fall   run   wake

Helpful words

ran drank ate
held found made
woke fell

2 Write these sentences, as if they had happened in the past:

Tom <u>is eating</u> his toast quickly.

He <u>is drinking</u> his milk as fast as possible.

It <u>is making</u> him feel ill!

Tip

You need to swap a verb in the **Helpful words** box for the words underlined.

Sentence work

- To understand and use speech marks

 Remember

Put the speech marks carefully before and after the words actually spoken.

Speech marks

"Where is Tom?" said Mum.

Remember, " " are called **speech marks**. They show us the words people said.

1 Copy these sentences, and put in the missing speech marks:

Where is Tom? said Mum.

I wish I was still in bed, mumbled Tom.

Come on Tom! We are waiting for you! said his teacher.

2 Finish this sentence:

"I'm late because ——————," said Tom.

 Word work

- To learn to spell words with *wh*

Helpful words

Who   Which   When
What   Where

 Remember

Questions must end with a **question mark (?)**.

wh words

"Where is Tom?" said Mum.

Often **question words** begin with **wh**.

1 Write the missing **wh** question words for each of these answers:

Q When does the story of Tom begin?
A The story of Tom begins in the morning, before school.

Q ————— room is Tom in?
A Tom is in his bedroom.

Q ————— is calling Tom?
A Tom's mum is calling him.

2 Write the questions for these answers:

Tom wishes he was still in bed!

Tom gets to school at three minutes past nine.

How we say things

We often use the word **said**:

"Tom, time to get up. Breakfast is ready," said Mum.

Sometimes we can use more interesting words than **said**:

"Tom, time to get up. Breakfast is ready," grumbled Mum.

Word work

● To pick out dialogue words

Remember

Dialogue words show **how** we say things.

1 Choose a different word to fill the gap.
You are not allowed to use **said**.

"Where is Tom? He is going to be late,"
_____ Mum.

"Tom, are you up yet?" _____ Mum.

"Tom!" _____ Mum.

"I wish I was still in bed," _____ Tom.

"Come on, Tom, we are waiting for you,"
_____ his teacher.

Helpful words

yelled grumbled sighed
mumbled shouted called
complained asked

2 Make a list of as many words as you can that could
sometimes be used instead of **said**.

Letter patterns

I wonder
where Tom is?

Handwriting

wh wh wh wh wh wh wh wh wh

1 Copy the **wh** letter pattern.

2 a Add wh to these letters to make some words:

where ___ich ___at ___y ___en

b Copy this neatly:
Tom's teacher asked why he was
late and where he'd been.

The Telly is Watching You

Sentence work

● To use verbs with similar meanings

Remember

Words with similar meanings are called **synonyms**.

Helpful words

chuckle   hobble   grip
giggle   stroll   snigger
grab   grasp   march
cackle   amble   clutch

Choosing verbs

Some verbs have **meanings** that are nearly the same:

watch   look   glance   stare

All of these verbs are about the way we look at something, but each has a slightly different meaning.

1 Write at least four verbs in each column.

Holding verbs	Laughing verbs	Walking verbs
grip	chuckle	hobble

2 Write another verb that has a similar meaning to each of these:

push _shove_   cry   hit

love   eat   relax

shout   throw

Speech marks

Ben said, "You always want things your own way!"

1 Copy the words that were actually spoken in these sentences:

"Try another channel," she said, through a mouthful of cake. "This is awful."

"Rotten old horses," said Shani. "Who needs them?"

And Shani sang, "Boring, boring, boring!"

2 Think of when you last had an argument with someone. Write the conversation, using speech marks.

Remember

" " are called **speech marks**. They show us the words people said.

Helpful words

shouted   mumbled
yelled   muttered
cried   screamed

oi and *oy* words

point

coin

boy

toy

Say the words in the picture.
Listen to the sound the *oi* and *oy* letters make.

Word work

● To learn to spell words with *oi* and *oy*

1 Choose an *oi* or *oy* word to match each picture:

Helpful words

coin boil toy enjoy
joint point

2 Underline the letters that make the same sound in each word you have written for question 1, like this:

toy   point

23

Word work

- To learn the suffix *ful*

 Remember

A **suffix** is a group of letters added to the end of a word.

Suffixes

Shani talk**ed** with a mouth**ful** of cake.

ed and **ful** are suffixes.

1 Add the suffix *ful* to each of these words:

use *useful*	care
hope	wonder
help	pain
spite	thought

2 Write two sentences, each using a word with the suffix *ful*.

 Handwriting

Letter patterns

Rotten old horses!

ot ol ot ol ot ol ot ol ot ol ot

1 Copy the **ot** and **ol** letter patterns.

2 a Add *ot* or *ol* to these letters to make some words:

r**ot**ten   l___tery   g___den   f___ded   c___ton

b Copy this neatly:

"The lottery is better than rotten old horses!" said Shani.

Party Time!

Adjectives

Adjectives are **describing words**.
They tell us about nouns.

adjective noun   **adjective** noun

<u>yellow</u> butter   <u>hot</u> oven

Sentence work

● To understand and use adjectives

1 Adjectives can tell us about size, shape and colour. Write an adjective to describe each of these nouns:

_____ balloons

_____ bar of chocolate

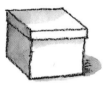

_____ box

_____ trainers

Remember

Nouns are name words for things, people or places.

Helpful words

square red
blue huge

2 Sometimes we need two adjectives to describe a noun. Write a **size** adjective and a **colour** adjective to describe each of five things in the picture. One is done to help you.

<u>tall</u> <u>red</u> candle   _____ _____ ball

_____ _____ trousers   _____ _____ cake

_____ _____ dress

Helpful words

tall red blue big
orange small yellow
white large long

25

Sentence work

- To use punctuation marks at the end of sentences

Ending sentences

We use a **full stop** (.) to end most sentences, but we use a **question mark** (?) when a question is asked.
We use an **exclamation mark** (!) when something is very important, or someone is cross or surprised, or something happens suddenly.

Take care!   Hey, stop that!   Ouch!

 Tip

Notice that **?** and **!** both have a full stop built into them.

1 Copy these, and add the missing punctuation marks:

Ouch, I've cut my finger
Where is the honey
Mum, come quickly
What time is Ben coming
Beware

2 Write two sentences of your own about Carl's party. One must finish with a question mark and one with an exclamation mark.

 Word work

- To learn to spell words with *or* and *ore*

or and *ore* words

cornflakes   store

 Tip

Say the words. Listen to the sound the letters **or** and **ore** make.

1 Write at least three words in each column, and more if you can.

or words	ore words
fork	snore

2 Write a sentence that has an **or** word and an **ore** word.

Helpful words

more   fork   storm
horn   snore   core
born   shore   store

26

Syllables

Say these words out loud.
Listen carefully to the beats in
each word.

cornflakes = *corn/flakes*
        1 beat 1 beat
Each part of the word you have
said is a **syllable**.

 Word work

● To understand syllables

Tip

Clap the beats as you say
the words.

Remember

It is easier to hear the
syllables if you clap as
you say the word.

1 Copy each word. Put a line between each syllable,
like this:

butter has 2 syllables   *but/ter*
cornflakes has 2 syllables
coconut has 3 syllables
sugar has 2 syllables
oats has 1 syllable
honey has 2 syllables

2 Write four more words with three syllables.

Pattern practice

 Handwriting

an en in on un an en in on un

1 Neatly copy the letter patterns in the box three times.

2 Add one of the letter patterns to make these letters
into words:

h—d   t—t   p—   p—d

b—   b—d   h—   b—

Robin Hood Meets Little John

Sentence work

- To understand singular and plural

Singular and plural

Singular means **one** and **plural** means **more than one**.

rabbit
singular

rabbits
plural

Remember

Most **plural nouns** have **s** on the end.

1 Write the plural of each of these singular nouns:

hut huts   castle   bow   arrow
bridge   camp   forest   tree

2 Write the singular of each of these nouns:

cloaks cloak   horses   frogs   apples
feasts   friends   tables   pies

Using I and me

> When we write about ourselves,
> we use the words **I** and **me**.
> The little word **I** must *always* be a capital letter.

1 Copy these sentences correctly into your book.
Put in all the missing capital letters.

i have always liked the story of robin hood.
my brother nathan and i sometimes play robin
hood and little john. nathan lets me be little
john as i am bigger than him. he is smaller
than me so he is robin. one day uncle paul
helped us to make bows and arrows, but aunty
tina said they were too dangerous and took
them away!

2 Add one more sentence of your own.

Words ending in *nch* and *tch*

1 How many actions can you find ending in **nch** or **tch**
in the picture.

2 Add *ed* to these words:

punch_   pinch_   scratch_   stretch_

Sentence work

● To correctly use the word *I*

Remember

People's names always
start with a capital letter.
Don't forget to start
sentences with a capital
letter.

Word work

● To learn to spell words
with *nch* and *tch*

Helpful words

punch pinch itch
stretch stitch scratch

29

Word work

- To learn some spelling rules for plurals

Remember

Plural means more than one.

Tip

Some words need **s** and some need to have **es** added.

Handwriting

Special plural spellings

If a noun ends in **ch**, **sh**, **s** or **x** es is added to make it plural.

branch   *bran<u>ches</u>*

1 Write these nouns as plurals:

ditch	*scratch*	*crash*	*box*
bush	*dress*	*kiss*	*fox*

2 Write these nouns as plurals:

rabbit	*church*	*brush*	*bridge*
horse	*stick*	*cloak*	*saddle*

Pattern practice

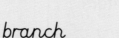

ar ai ar ai ar ai ar ai ar ai ar ai ar ai

1 Neatly copy the letter patterns in the box three times.

2 Add one of the letter patterns to make these letters into words:

st____   c____t   b____k   h____p

m____d   r____n   sn____l   t____l

The Dragon and the Cockerel

Choosing adjectives

> Some adjectives have **similar meanings**:
>
> big large huge enormous
>
> All of these adjectives describe how large something is, but each has a slightly different meaning.

1 Sort these adjectives into two columns:

> sad splendid miserable
> lovely downcast gorgeous
> unhappy attractive depressed
> beautiful mournful pretty

 **Remember**

Words with similar meanings are called **synonyms**.

Adjectives describing sadness	Adjectives describing good looks

2 Copy these sentences, choosing a better adjective than the words underlined:

Dragon was feeling <u>very sad</u>.

He wished he was a <u>pretty</u> dragon.

If only he had something on his head everyone would say he was <u>pretty</u>.

Poor dragon felt even more <u>unhappy</u> when he saw the <u>pretty</u> cockerel.

Sentence work

- To correctly use the words *am*, *is* and *are*

Using am, is and are

We use **am** with the word I:
"*I am miserable*," *said Dragon.*
We use **is** with one person or thing:
"*Dragon is very sad today*," *said Cockerel.*
We use **are** with more than one person or thing:
"*We are sorry he is so unhappy*," *said all the other creatures.*

1 Copy these sentences.
Write *am*, *is* or *are* in each gap.

"*I __ unlucky not to have antlers*," *said Dragon.*
"*Cockerel __ the person I must talk to*," *he said to himself.*
"*Why __ you all staring at me?*" *he grumbled to the other creatures.*
"*We __ not staring*," *they said.*
"*Where __ Cockerel?*" *he asked Rabbit.*
"*I __ not sure*," *answered the little animal.*

2 Write your own sentence that has both *am* and *is* in it.

Word work

- To learn to spell words with *aw*

aw words

The dragon had the claws of an eagle.

1 Copy the sentences.
Fill the gap with an **aw** word.

The dragon woke up and gave a big _____.
He was lying on a bed of _____.
The dragon _____ out of bed.
He looked in his _____ for a clean pair of socks.

2 List as many words as you can that have the **aw** pattern.

Helpful words

*crawled   straw   drawer
dawn   yawn   lawn*

Adding *er* and *est* to describing words

 Word work

The dragon's great**est** shame was that he had nothing on top of his head.

great   greater   greatest

- To understand how words change when *er* and *est* are added

1 Copy the table. Fill in the missing words.

	Add er	Add est
short	shorter	shortest
tall		
small		
long		
weak		
kind		

2 Write a sentence using one **er** word and one **est** word.

Pattern practice

 Handwriting

aw au aw au aw au aw au aw au

1 Neatly copy the letter patterns in the box three times.

2 Copy these clues. Next to each one write the answer using an **aw** or **au** word.

a grassy area in a garden
a boy's name beginning with P
an eagle has two, the dragon had four
used for cutting wood
tomato _____ tastes good with chips

Helpful words

Paul   saw   sauce
claws   lawn

33

Firefighters to the Rescue

Sentence work

- To understand how words change when *er* and *est* are added

Comparing adjectives

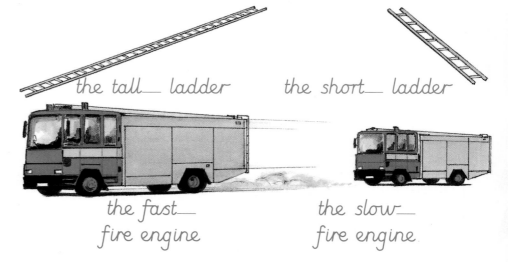

When we compare **two** things, we add *er* to an adjective:

This is a <u>long</u> ladder.

Yes, but this one is long<u>er</u>.

When we compare **more than two** things, we add *est* to an adjective:

There are three <u>long</u> ladders.

Quick! Get me the long<u>est</u> one!

Remember

Word endings are called **suffixes**.

1 Choose the correct endings for these adjectives:

the tall__ ladder   the short__ ladder

the fast__ fire engine   the slow__ fire engine

the strong__ firefighter   the weak__ firefighter

2 Write a sentence which has an *er* and an *est* adjective in it.

Capital letters in titles

We use **capital letters** for the first and **all the important words** in a title.

Firefighters to the Rescue

 Sentence work

- To use capital letters in titles

1 Copy these titles, adding the missing capital letters:

a day in the life of a firefighter

the great escape

an encyclopedia of fire engines

firefighters through the ages

so you want to be a firefighter

2 Make up a title for a book about the history of fire engines.

Tip

Short words such as *a*, *an*, *be*, *and*, *for*, *in*, *of*, *on*, *the* and *to* are **not** important words in titles.

ph words

Say the word tele**ph**one out loud.
Listen to the sound the ***ph*** makes.

telephone

 Word work

- To learn to spell words with *ph*

1 Write a ***ph*** word to match each picture.

Helpful words

microphone   dolphin
photograph   alphabet
sphere   elephant

2 Write a funny, silly sentence that has as many ***ph*** words as possible.

Word work

- To learn the suffixes *ful* and *less*

Remember

A **suffix** is added to the end of a word to make a new word.

 Handwriting

Suffixes

The *helpful* firefighter *helped* the *helpless* old lady.

ful, **ed** and **less** are all **suffixes**

help + ful = helpful
help + ed = helped
help + less = helpless

helpless   helpful

1 Add the suffixes *ful* and *less* to each of these words to make new words:

hope   helpful   helpless

use   care   pain   thought

2 Copy these words. Underline the suffix. Then write the word before the suffix was added, like this:

hopeless   hope<u>less</u>   hope

faithful   useless   happened   wonderful

Pattern practice

ou ow ou ow ou ow ou ow ou ow ou ow

1 Neatly copy the letter patterns in the box three times.

2 Add one of the letter patterns to make these letters into words:

h___se   cl___d   sh___t   sp___t

d___n   t___n   ___l   cr___d

Saint George and the Dragon

Collective nouns

> A **collective noun** is the special name for a collection of people, places or things.
>
> a *flock* of sheep   a *crowd* of people

1 Copy these two lists. Draw lines to link them.

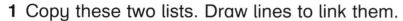

Noun	Collective noun
cows	team
bees	flock
sheep	herd
trees	bunch
players	swarm
flowers	forest

2 Copy these sentences. Choose the correct collective noun from the brackets.

A (mob, flock) of birds flew overhead.

The (team, crowd) of people watched.

One woman held a (swarm, bundle) of sticks.

Helpful words

team

flock

herd

bunch

swarm

forest

37

Sentence work

- To understand that proper nouns need capital letters

Remember

Proper nouns are **special naming words**.

Proper nouns need capital letters

> **Proper nouns** always start with capital letters:
> Saint George   England
> The names of **days** and **months** are proper nouns:
> Sunday   Friday   May   June

1 Copy just the proper nouns, giving each one a capital letter:

> monday   dragon   princess   friday   july
> prince   harry   saint george   wednesday

2 Copy these sentences, putting in the missing capital letters:

> it was the last friday in april when the lots were drawn.
>
> old mrs potter was scared that her grandchild, william, might be fed to the dragon.
>
> saint george arrived just in time.

Word work

- To learn to spell words with *are* and *ere*

are and *ere* words

The letters **ere** and **are** sometimes make the same sound in words.

Where is the town square?

1 Write an **are** or **ere** word to match each picture:

2 Write *there* and *where*, each in a sentence about Saint George and the dragon.

Helpful words

spare   care   hare
stare   scare   share

Joining words

Sometimes two words like **do** and **not** are joined together to make one word.

When these words are joined together a letter is squeezed out.

do not = don't

o has been squeezed out.
The **'** shows where it was.

Word work
- To understand when an apostrophe is needed

1 Join these words together.
In all these words the **o** in **not** must be squeezed out.

do not = don't   *did not =*
was not =   *have not =*
should not =   *would not =*

Tip

' is called an **apostrophe**.

2 Which two words were these made from?

isn't = is not   *they're*
I'm   *it's*
you're   *we're*

Remember

Do not forget the **'**.

Pattern practice

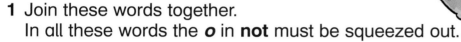

wa wa wa wa wa wa wa wa wa wa

Handwriting

1 Neatly copy the letter pattern in the box three times.

2 Think of a **wa** word to answer these riddles.
Write the answers neatly.
a big white bird, that rhymes with **gone**

a magic stick, that rhymes with **pond**

between hot and cold, and rhymes with **storm**

makes you clean, and rhymes with **posh**

marshy land, that rhymes with **romp**

Helpful words

*warm   wash   swan
swamp   wand*

The Good Friend

Sentence work

- To understand when sentences are singular and plural

Singular and plural sentences

Words can be changed from **singular** to **plural**, and so can whole sentences.
To change sentences we change some, but not all, of the words.

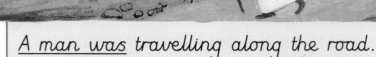

A man was travelling along the road.

Some men were travelling along the road.

 1 Change these from **singular** to **plural**.
Underline the words you have changed.

A robber attacked the man.

A holy man was coming along the road.

He decided not to stop.

He said he was in a hurry.

2 Now copy these sentences, changing them from **plural** to **singular**.
Underline the words you have changed.

Some men stopped to help.

They were very kind and thoughtful.

Soon they had bandaged the wounds.

They were good friends indeed!

Words that go together

> Some words often go together.
> *I am   you are   he is   they are*

1 Copy the sentences. Fill the gaps with *am*, *is* or *are*.

"I ____ lucky to be alive," thought the man.

"They ____ not going to help me," he muttered.

"You ____ very kind," he said to the stranger.

"I ____ only doing what you would do," he replied.

"He ____ badly injured," the stranger told the inn-keeper.

2 Write these sentences correctly.

I is sure they am going to help.

You am kinder than they is.

I are staying until you is well again.

Silent letters

> In some words, not all the letters have a sound. These letters are called **silent letters**.
> *wrist*
> *knife*

1 Copy these words. Underline the silent letters.

a *wrong   write   wring*
b *knife   knock   knit*
c *lamb   climb   crumb*

2 Find one more word to go with each set. The pictures give you some clues.

Remember

Do not forget the speech marks.

Tip

Look carefully at the words underlined!

 Word work

● To learn to spell words with silent letters

Tip

Say each word aloud – it will help you find the silent letter.

Word work

● To understand what an antonym is

Remember

Antonym is another name for **opposite**.

Helpful words

nonsense   illegal
invisible   impossible
dishonest   incorrect
impatient   dislike

Opposites

> Most antonyms are **different words**:
> empty full   up down
> but some antonyms are made by **adding a prefix**:
> happy <u>un</u>happy   obey <u>dis</u>obey

1 Copy these two lists of words.
Draw a line to match the antonyms.

alive   dirty
black   easy
clean   there
difficult   dead
here   white

2 Add a prefix to make antonyms for these words.
Underline each prefix.

correct   visible   like   honest
possible   patient   sense   legal

Handwriting

wrestle
wrap
wreck
wren

Pattern practice

wr wr wr wr wr wr wr wr wr wr wr wr

1 Neatly copy the letter pattern in the box three times.

2 Find and copy the nine **wr** words hidden in the puzzle box.

w	r	i	s	t	y	d
r	w	r	e	n	l	x
o	w	r	e	c	k	w
n	f	w	r	a	p	r
g	w	r	i	n	g	o
s	w	r	i	t	e	t
w	r	e	s	t	l	e

Making a Musical Instrument

Overworked words

- To replace overworked words with better words

Some words are used too much.

nice   lots   got   good

That was a nice tune.

It is nice to come to the school concert.

He's wearing a nice jacket.

She is a nice teacher.

This is a nice cup of tea.

1 In the picture, everyone is using the word **nice**. Write the sentences again, choosing a word instead of nice in each sentence.

2 Copy these sentences, finding an adjective better than **good** for each sentence:

She is a good drummer.

That is a good picture.

It is good to see Mum enjoying the music.

Helpful words

clever   brilliant
special   talented
beautiful   delightful

43

Sentence work

● To use fewer words

Too many words

Often we use **too many words**.

It will be a really really good parents' concert that we are putting on for all our mums and dads and grandmas and grandads tomorrow afternoon after lunch. (28 words)

It will be an excellent concert that we perform tomorrow afternoon for our families. (14 words)

1 Write these sentences using fewer words:

The concert was really really <u>good</u>. There were <u>lots of</u> people there, and our head teacher said lots and lots of <u>nice</u> things about it afterwards and we all <u>got</u> a big clap at the end of it all.

2 Write another word that could have been used instead for each of the words underlined in question 1.

Word work

● To learn to spell words with *er*, *ir* and *ur*

er, ir and ur words

Tip

Say the words below. Listen to the sound the letters **er**, **ir** and **ur** make.

bird   nurse
church   shirt

1 Look at the picture.
Copy and fill the gap in these sentences:

The ___ landed on the top of the girl's head.
One child is dressed up as a ___.
We can see the ___ through the window.
The boy's ___ is very bright.

2 Write two more **er**, **ir** and **ur** words.

Alphabetical order

Words in a dictionary are put in the same order as the letters in the alphabet.

a b c d e f g h i j k l m n o p q r s t u v w x y z
If the first letters of the words are the same, look at the **second letter** in each word.

 tambourine  trumpet tuba

1 Write these groups of words in alphabetical order. The first one is done to help you.

triangle cymbals drum   cymbals drum triangle
hall classroom playground
teacher parents caretaker
playing singing dancing

2 Write these groups of words in alphabetical order. The first one is done to help you.

song singer shaker   shaker singer song
brother baby boy
Julie Jamie Joel
clapping cheering calling

Pattern practice

al ul al ul al ul al ul al ul al ul al ul

1 Neatly copy the letter patterns in the box three times.

2 Add al or ul to make these letters into words:

____ways   usef____   ____so   helpf____
____ready   caref____   painf____   ____most

 Word work

- To practise ordering words alphabetically

 Remember

We say that the words in dictionaries are in **alphabetical order**.

 Remember

You need to look at the **first letter** of each word.

 Tip

You will need to look at the **second** letters too.

 Handwriting

Helpful words

always also already
almost useful helpful
careful painful

45

Gulliver's Travels

Sentence work

- To use better words in the past tense

Using did and done

> If something has *already happened*, it happened in the **past**.
>
> *Gulliver <u>did</u> his best to escape.*
>
> *The little people <u>had done</u> their best to stop him escaping.*
>
> We use **did** by itself, but **done** usually needs to be close to **had**, **has** or **have**.

1 Copy these sentences.
Fill the gaps with *did* or *done*.

The little people _____ not want to hurt Gulliver.

Gulliver wondered what he had _____ to upset them.

"What have I _____ to upset you?" he asked.

He _____ his best to pull himself free.

They had _____ a good job fixing him down.

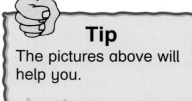

Tip
The pictures above will help you.

2 Write two sentences about Gulliver, one using *did* and the other using *done*.

Writing letters

Here is the start of a letter from one of the little people to his uncle.

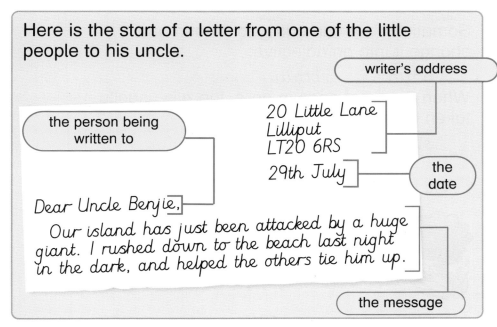

writer's address

the person being written to

20 Little Lane
Lilliput
LT20 6RS

29th July

the date

Dear Uncle Benjie,

Our island has just been attacked by a huge giant. I rushed down to the beach last night in the dark, and helped the others tie him up.

the message

1 Copy the letter so far, and finish the message.

2 Write the beginning of a letter, using your own address.
Write today's date under the address.
Write *Dear* _____, and write the name of someone you might like to write a letter to.

str words

1 Write five words that begin with the letters *str*.

2 Put each **str** word in a sentence like this:

stream *They brought buckets of water from the stream for Gulliver to drink.*

Sentence work

● To practise writing letters

Tip

Make up a name for the little person. Write about how he might have felt.

Word work

● To learn to spell words with *str*

Helpful words

stream   street
string   straw
strain   strong

47

Word work

- To understand how words change when *y* is added

Remember

Nouns are **names** of things, people or places.

Adjectives are **describing** words. They tell us about nouns.

Tip

Watch out for the words that end in *e*.

Adding *y*

Sometimes we can add **y** to a noun and change it into an adjective:

brain　　brainy

When the word ends in an **e**, the **e** is usually taken off before the **y** is added:

slime　　slimy

1 Add *y* to each of these words:

smoke

rain

stone

sleep

leaf

nose

2 Write the adjectives again, this time adding a noun, like this:

smoky fire

Handwriting

Pattern practice

ch sh ch sh ch sh ch sh ch sh ch sh

1 Neatly copy the letter patterns in the box three times.

2 Make as many words as you can by adding *ch* or *sh* to each of these word endings.
Write your answers neatly in two lists.

＿＿eep　＿＿op　＿＿ick　＿＿ut　＿＿ed　＿＿in

＿＿ell　＿＿ips　＿＿imp　＿＿rimp　＿＿est

The Tale of Thomas Mead

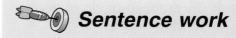

Pronouns

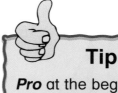

- To understand and use pronouns

> A *pronoun* can be used **in place of a noun**.
> Here are some pronouns we often use:
>
> *I   you   him   it   she   he   they*
>
> "Why should I?" Thomas Mead replied.
> I in this sentence is used in place of Thomas Mead.

Tip

Pro at the beginning of a word can mean *in place of*.

1 Copy these sentences, but write pronouns in place of the words underlined:

"<u>Thomas Mead</u> doesn't want to read," said the teacher.

<u>Thomas Mead</u> couldn't read notices.

<u>The workmen</u> were painting.

"Can't <u>Thomas Mead</u> read?" the workmen cried.

2 Copy the two pronouns in each of these sentences:

She wished he could read.

They said he was stupid walking there.

It could have hit him on the head.

You should listen to what she says.

DANGER
workmen
overhead

49

Sentence work

- To practise using speech marks

Word work

- To learn to spell words with *ea*

Helpful words

bread   team   head
thread   feather   dream
beam   read   each   lead

Speech marks

"I wish you would!" his teacher sighed.
" " are called **speech marks**.
They show us the words people said.

1 Copy the words that were **actually spoken** in these sentences:

"I wish you would!" his teacher sighed.

"Why should I?" Thomas Mead replied.

"Can't you read?" the workmen cried.

2 Copy these sentences, putting in the missing speech marks:

Run to the shops for me please, said Mum.

But I'm watching telly, said the boy.

Don't worry then, but there won't be any tea tonight! she replied.

ea words

Say the word overh**ea**d.
Listen to the sound *ea* makes.

Say Thomas M**ea**d.
Listen to the sound *ea* makes.

DANGER
workmen
overhead

1 Find five *ea* words to go in each of these two columns. Two have been done to help you.

ea sounds like overhead	ea sounds like Thomas Mead
bread	team

2 What do you notice about the words **read** and **lead**?

50

Dialogue words

"Can't you read?" the workmen <u>cried</u>.
The words **called** and **shouted** could be used instead of **cried**.

● To use dialogue words

1 Write two synonyms for the dialogue words in **bold** in each of these sentences:

"I wish you would learn to read, Thomas," his teacher **sighed**.

"Why should I?" **replied** Thomas.

"You wouldn't get paint in your hair," **giggled** his friend.

"But learning to read is hard," **muttered** Thomas.

"It can be fun as well," **said** his teacher.

Remember

Dialogue words tell how we say things.

Synonyms are words with similar meanings.

2 Make two columns:
quiet dialogue words, like **whispered**
loud dialogue words, like **called**

Quiet	Loud

Helpful words

yelled grumbled sighed
muttered shouted called
complained laughed
joked cried whispered

Pattern practice

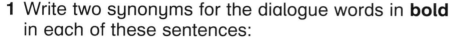

it et it et it et it et it et it et it et it et

1 Neatly copy the letter patterns in the box three times.

2 Add one of the letter patterns to make these letters into words:

buck___   *b___*   *tick___*   *wick___*

l___   *rock___*   *s___*   *jack___*

Children in Roman Times

 Sentence work

- To understand and use possessive pronouns

Remember

A **pronoun** can be used **in place of a noun**.
Here are some:

I   you   him   it
she   he   they.

Possessive pronouns

Some pronouns are called **possessive pronouns**:

his   hers   mine   ours   theirs   yours

They tell us who owns something.

This hoop is Alex's hoop.
This hoop is his.

his = possessive pronoun for Alex's hoop.

1 Write a possessive pronoun that could be used for the words in bold:

I've broken **my hoop**, so can I use **your hoop**?

You say it is **your slate**, but I think it is **my slate**!

Their school is bigger, but it isn't as good as **our school**.

2 Write a sentence using each pair of possessive pronouns:

yours, mine   hers, ours   theirs, his

Joining sentences

> Words that we use to join sentences are called **conjunctions**.
>
> *We had wrestling lessons. I prefer fencing.*
> *We had wrestling lessons <u>but</u> I prefer fencing.*

1 Join these sentences with *but* or *and*:

The boys from rich families went to school. The girls stayed at home.

The Romans built baths for washing and swimming. They also met their friends there.

2 Write the two sentences that this sentence was made from:

I read stories to my little sister and she shows me the pictures she has drawn.

ch words

1 Say the words.
Make a list of the words that have the same *ch* sound as in **school**.

anchor	*stomach*	*echo*
teacher	*choir*	*ache*
Christmas	*chick*	*chorus*

2 Write eight words with *ch* as it sounds in **chair**.

Sentence work

● To understand and use conjunctions

Tip

Conjunctions are sometimes called **joining words**.

Word work

● To learn to spell words with *ch*

Tip

The letters *ch* can make two very different sounds.

Word work

- To practise using a dictionary

 Tip

A **dictionary** has *meanings of words* and helps us to *check our spellings.*

 Remember

Another name for meaning is **definition**.

Dictionary work

Ss

scarf a piece of material worn around the neck

school a place where children learn

scissors a tool that can cut

scream a loud cry

seagull a bird that often lives near the sea

1 Look at the information in the dictionary above. Answer these questions:

Why does a **seagull** have its name?

What is the meaning of **scream**?

Is this spelling of **scisors** correct?

In this dictionary, which word comes before **school**?

2 Look in a dictionary.
Find three more words that begin with **s** and copy their meanings.

 Handwriting

 **Helpful words**

cold   hold
fold   gold

Pattern practice

1 Neatly copy the letter pattern in the box three times.

2 Think of an **old** word to answer each clue.

a very valuable metal

the antonym for hot

where cargo is kept on a ship

to flap something over neatly

to grip something with your hand

Superpooch

Male or female?

We often use different words for writing about males and females.

Girl, *she*, *her* are **female words**.

Boy, *he*, *him* are **male words**.

1 Copy this list of nouns.
Next to the **male** words write M and next to the **female** words write F.

girl   boy   mother   aunt   grandmother
bull   son   princess   king   actress
Mrs May   Chatwin   Poochie

2 Copy this table.
Find pronouns to write in the columns.

Male	Female	Can be male or female

 Sentence work

• To understand male and female words

Tip

Words that tell us whether a person or animal is male or female are called **gender words**.

Helpful words

she   he   they   it   you
I   her   hers   yours   his
theirs   mine   me
him   we   ours

Sentence work

- To learn, in speech marks, the place of the comma

Speech marks and commas

"I love my little dog," said Mrs May.

" " are called **speech marks**.

They show us the words people said.

We also usually put a comma at the end of the words spoken.

"His name is Poochie," she added.

1 Copy these sentences, adding the missing speech marks and commas:

Poochie has a little tail said Mrs May.

He and Chatwin are good friends she said.

They often play together she added.

2 Write one more sentence that Mrs May might have said about her two pets.

Word work

- To learn to spell words with *ear* and *ead*

ear and *ead* words

Poochie has long ears and a big head.

Say the words.

Listen to the different sound the letters **ea** make in the two words.

Helpful words

spear   year   bread
clear   bedspread   dead
near   beard

1 Copy this table. Find words for each column.

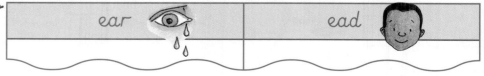

ear	ead

2 Write one sentence that has both an **ear** and an **ead** word in it.

Homonyms

- To understand and use homonyms

Some words have the **same spelling** but **different meanings**.

My dad has a hairy chest.
In the treasure chest there was some gold.

These words are called **homonyms**.

Remember

Definition means **meaning**.

1 Look carefully at the picture. List all the homonyms you can see.

2 Write two definitions of the word **row**.

Pattern practice

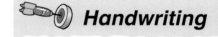 **Handwriting**

wh wh wh wh wh wh wh wh wh wh

1 Neatly copy the letter pattern in the box three times.

2 Neatly write a **wh** word for each picture.

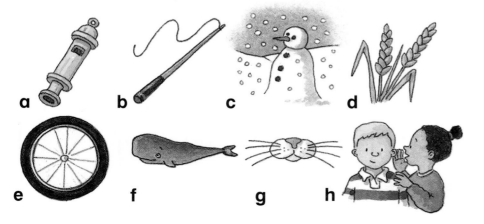

a   b   c   d

e   f   g   h

Helpful words

white   whip
whistle   whale
whisker   wheat
wheel   whisper

Fun Poems

Sentence work

● To know when to use *I* and *me*

Tip

Pronouns used instead of people's names are called **personal pronouns**.

Helpful words

his   hers   mine   ours
theirs   yours   I   you
him   she   he   they
me   we   them

Remember

I always has a capital letter.

Personal pronouns

When we write about **ourselves** we use the pronouns like **I** and **me**:

I like tongue twisters.

When we write about **other people** we use pronouns like **you** and **they**:

Have you ever seen a dog dig and a duck dive?

1 Make two columns of personal pronouns.

Pronouns about me	Pronouns about others

2 Copy this sentence and underline the personal pronouns:

José and I are going to his house to ask if he is allowed to come with me to the library to borrow a book of tongue twisters.

BILL BIGGA'S BLUE BUSES
BEAT BLOGGS' BROWN BUSES

GO BY BLOGGS

BIGGA TRANSPORT

BLOGGS' BROWN BUSES

Capital letters in poetry

We nearly always use a
capital letter for the beginning
of each new line in a poem.

<u>D</u>ick had a dog
<u>T</u>he dog dug
<u>T</u>he dog dug deep
<u>H</u>ow deep did Dick's dog dig?

1 Copy a verse of a poem that you like.
Don't forget the capital letters at the beginning of
each line.

2 Write another verse yourself for the poem
you have copied.

Collecting double letters

1 Some letters often come together in pairs. Choose
either *ss*, *ll*, *ff* or *tt* to finish each of these words:

te___   cro___   bo___le   sku___

we___   sti___   ke___le   pre___ing

fu___   be___y   ba___le   dre___

fi___ing   li___le   le___er   o___

2 Finish these words. The answers all have a double
letter.

k_____ used to boil water

l_____ another word for small

s_____ the bones in your head

o_____ opposite of on

c_____ to be upset

b_____ two armies fighting

 Sentence work

● To practise using capital
letters in poetry

 **Word work**

● To learn to spell some
words with double letters

Tip

All the answers are in
question 1.

Word work

- To learn the rule about adding the suffix *er*

Remember

The vowel letters are
a e i o u.

Adding *er*

When we add *er* to a word, remember the rule.
If there is a **single vowel letter before the last letter**, the **last letter is doubled** before adding *er*.

flap flapper

vowel letter

Penguin
Big flapp**er**
Belly tapp**er**
Big splash**er**
Fish catch**er**
Beak snapp**er.**

1 Look at the **er** words in this poem.
Make a list of the root words that have had their last letter doubled before **er** was added.

Tip

A **root word** is the small word before any prefixes or suffixes are added.

2 Add *er* to these words:

catch + er = catcher

flap	*splash*
thin	*near*
clap	*trap*
fat	*big*

Handwriting

Pattern practice

oth oth oth oth oth oth oth oth oth oth

1 Neatly copy the letter patterns in the box three times.

2 Copy this tongue twister as neatly as you can:

My mother says her mother's brother is meaner than her brother's mother.

Road Accident

Pronouns and contractions

A **contraction** is used in place of two words.
We use ' to show where letters are missing.

I am so sorry!

I'm so sorry!

1 Many contractions have pronouns in them.
Copy these pairs of words. Underline the pronoun, and then write a contraction next to the pair.
The first is done to help you.

I am = I'm

we are   he is   you will   they are

I will   she is   they will

2 Copy these contractions.
Underline the pronoun in each one.

we're = we're

he's   I'll   she's   they're

I'm   you're   you'll

 Sentence work

● To shorten words that follow pronouns

 Remember

' is called an **apostrophe**.

 Tip

When something gets smaller, it **contracts**.

 Remember

A **pronoun** stands in place of a noun.

Sentence work

- To join short sentences to make them more interesting

Remember

Conjunctions are sometimes called **joining words**.

Helpful words

and but so because although though after for until yet then as or when while so

Word work

- To learn to spell words with *igh*

Helpful words

night thigh right light fight high

Using conjunctions

Conjunctions help us to write longer, more interesting sentences.

We live by a busy road. I'm always careful when I go to the shops.

We live by a busy road so I'm always careful when I go to the shops.

so is a conjunction in this sentence.

1 Join these pairs of sentences to make one sentence:

They were having a cup of tea. They heard a loud crash.

It was stupid of the driver to take his eyes off the road. He seemed very sorry.

2 Write the conjunction in each of these sentences:

I was about to cross the road when I saw a lorry coming very quickly.

The people in the café were badly shocked although they were lucky not to have been injured.

igh words

The people in the café had a big fr**igh**t when the lorry nearly hit them!

1 Write an *igh* word to match each picture:

Expressions

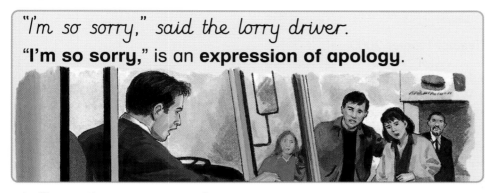

"I'm so sorry," said the lorry driver.

"I'm so sorry," is an **expression of apology**.

1 Copy these expressions.
Write what type of expression each one is.
The first one is done to help you.

"Watch out!" is an expression of warning.

"Hello"

"I'm very grateful"

"Wow!"

"Excuse me"

2 Now write another expression of each type.

Pattern practice

$$ol \quad ol \quad ol \quad ol \quad ol \quad ol \quad ol \quad ol \quad ol \quad ol \quad ol \quad ol$$

1 Neatly copy the letter pattern in the box three times.

2 Match an **ol** word to answer each clue.

a flag hangs from it

the yellow part of an egg

begins with b and goes with a nut

the antonym of young

a slow, gentle walk

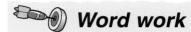

 Word work

- To think about and use some common expressions

Tip

Some reasons for **expressions**:

greeting   warning
apology   surprise
thanks

 **Handwriting**

Helpful words

*old   yolk   stroll
pole   bolt*

PEARSON EDUCATION LIMITED
Edinburgh Gate, Harlow, Essex, CM20 2JE, England
and Associated companies throughout the World.

First published 2000
Sixth impression 2005
© Hilary Frost, Sarah Lindsay and Heather Painter 2000

Printed in China
GCC/06

ISBN 0 582 40836 9

Acknowledgement

The handwriting characters in this book were created using *Handwriting for Windows 2.0*. This product enables the user to create model handwriting in the size, colour and style of their choice (including a dotted script). HfW2 runs on Windows 95 and above and is available from KBER (Kath Balcombe Educational Resources). Please contact Customer Services for details on 01743 356764.

Cover Bruce Coleman (Kim Taylor)

The publisher's policy is to use paper manufactured from sustainable forests.